WHERE IN ASIA IS MALAYSIA?

GEOGRAPHY LITERACY FOR KIDS
CHILDREN'S ASIA BOOKS

BABY PROFESSOR
EDUCATION KIDS

Speedy Publishing LLC

40 E. Main St. #1156

Newark, DE 19711

www.speedypublishing.com

Copyright 2017

In this book, we're going to talk about exploring the country of **Malaysia**. So, let's get right to it!

Malaysia is a melting pot of different types of populations and religions. Over 26 million people live in Malaysia, but it is sparsely populated for the amount of land it has. It is 329,750 square kilometers in size and is a little larger than the state of New Mexico.

WHERE IS MALAYSIA?

The country of Malaysia is located in southeastern Asia. It is composed of two completely separated landmasses with the South China Sea in between them.

The western section of Malaysia is located on the Malay Peninsula. Thailand is on its northern border and it surrounds the country of Singapore at its southern point. The Strait of Malacca waterway is west of this part of Malaysia.

The eastern section of Malaysia is located on the island of Borneo, but it is only a portion of the island. It is the northern portion and it includes the state of Sabah as well as the state of Sarawek. The southern portion of Borneo is part of the country of Indonesia. Malaysia also surrounds the tiny country of Brunei at the northern tip of the island of Borneo.

MAP OF MALAY PENINSULA
THAILAND
LANGKAWI
Kota Bahru
PERHENTIAN
LANG TENGAH
REDANG
DIDONG
PENANG
George Town
Kuala Terangganu
ANDAMAN SEA
Ipoh
KAPAS
TENGGOL
PANGKOR
MALAYSIA
Kuantan
STRAITS OF MALACCA
SOUTH CHINA SEA
Kuala Lumpur
Shah Alam
TIOMAN
Seremban
PEMANGGIL
AUR
Malacca
BESAR
Johor Baru
INDONESIA (SUMATRA)
SINGAPORE

WHAT ARE THE GEOGRAPHICAL AND NATURAL FEATURES OF MALAYSIA?

Each section of Malaysia has a different type of terrain. The Malay Peninsula has many areas of coastal plains that are located on its edges. On the west coast of the peninsula, facing the Strait of Malacca, there are a multitude of mangroves.

Mangroves have roots that live in salty, marshy tidal areas. The east coast of the peninsula has a rocky terrain with expansive beaches of sand. Hundreds of small islands are off the shore.

MANGROVES

MOUNT TAHAN

As you travel into the interior of the Malay Peninsula, the terrain gets more mountainous. There are hilly regions covered with rainforests and mountain ranges. There are three significant mountain ranges: The Titiwangsa, the Bintang, and the Tahan. The tallest peak is Mount Tahan, which has a height over 7,000 feet.

East Malaysia has some of the tallest mountains in the southeast region of Asia. The Crocker Mountain Range has the tallest mountain on the island of Borneo. It is Mount Kinabalu, which rises to a height of 13,455 feet.

MOUNT KINABALU

WHAT IS THE CLIMATE LIKE IN MALAYSIA?

Because Malaysia is near the equator, its climate is tropical. It's hot and very humid all year round. The average rainfall is about 98 inches every year and the typical temperature is about 80 degrees Fahrenheit. During the months of April to October there are monsoons in the southwest region and during the months of October to February there are monsoons in the northeast region.

WHAT IS THE CULTURE LIKE IN MALAYSIA?

Malaysia is truly a multicultural society. Many different ethnicities have lived there over the centuries. Malay people, Chinese people, and Indian people live and work harmoniously together although they differ greatly in terms of religion. The largest group of people is composed of the Malays.

MALAY GIRL WITH HEADGEAR

Their religion is Islam and they speak the Bahasa Malaysia language. They are the drivers of the politics in Malaysia. About 30% of the population is Chinese. The Chinese people own many of the businesses and are primarily Buddhists or Taoists. About 10% of the population consists of Indian citizens who are Hindus. Many different languages are spoken in the country, but the official language is Bahasa Malaysia. Many people living there speak English as well.

The music in Malaysia has been influenced by the Chinese culture as well as the Islamic. Lots of percussion instruments are used in Malaysian music, such as gongs, instruments made of shells, and the gendang, which is a type of drum. The traditional dances as well as dance dramas are a mixture of influences from Thailand, India, and Portugal.

GONG

The cuisine of Malaysia is a mixture of the different cultures of the country too. One dish that is uniquely Malaysian is satay, which consists of kebabs of chicken, pork, or beef accompanied by a peanut sauce that's spicy.

WHAT IS THE HISTORY OF MALAYSIA?

Evidence from archaeological digs shows that humans came to the landmasses of Malaysia over 40,000 years ago. By 1000 AD, the Malays had become the main race. They began what became the states of Malaysia and their culture was largely influenced by Indian culture.

MAJAPAHIT KINGDOM

From 100 to 300 AD, many different kingdoms sprang up across the lands. One of the major kingdoms was the empire of Langkasuka. From the late 7th century through the 13th century the Buddhist Srivijaya Empire ruled much of the Malay Peninsula. They controlled the surrounding waters and increased trade. They were the main power of the group of islands in the region. After the Srivijaya Empire fell, the Hindu Majapahit Kingdom gained control next.

The Hindus were followed by a Muslim ruling prince who established the state of Malacca around 1400 AD. The state of Malacca eventually became an important center for commerce.

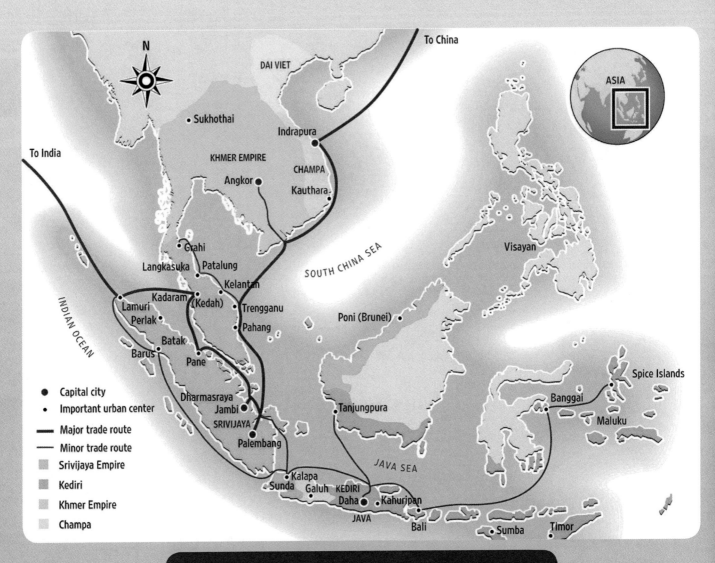

TRADE ROUTE IN SOUTHEAST ASIA

The European country of Portugal overthrew the state of Malacca in the year 1511 AD. This marked the first time that a power from Europe had access to the trade route in southeast Asia. Both the country of the Netherlands and the country of Spain took over in the 17th century.

In the middle of the 1800s, the area changed hands again. This time it was Britain that took over the rule of the country. The British recognized the wealth of natural resources in Malaysia and developed the rubber and tin industries. They ruled the country for 150 years until the outbreak of World War II when the land was invaded by Japanese soldiers.

After the Second World War was over, a federation was formed from the different territories that were ruled by the British. After a series of negotiations with Britain, Malaysia finally gained its independence in 1963. Singapore became a separate city-state in 1965.

From 1971 through the late 1990s, the country transformed from producing raw goods to an economy producing many different products including electronics.

WHAT PLACES ARE GOOD FOR EXPLORING IN MALAYSIA?

There are many beautiful places to explore in Malaysia. Here are a few places you might like to visit.

RAFFLESIA

Gunung Gading National Park

Would you like to see and smell the largest flower in the world? Then, you may want to visit the Gunung Gading National Park in the western area of East Malaysia on the island of Borneo. The rafflesia flower blooms there. It is over three feet wide and, unlike most flowers, it has a very stinky smell!

It generally blooms from the month of November until the month of January. There are numerous national parks in this area with beautiful beaches, scenic mountains, and dense jungles for exploring.

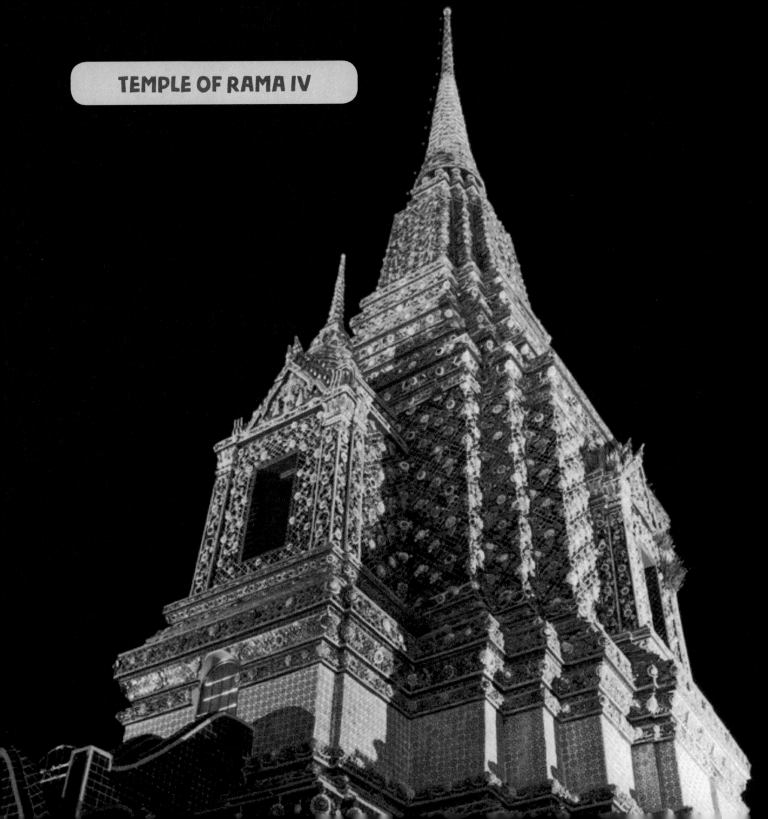
TEMPLE OF RAMA IV

Kek Lok Si Temple

Would you like to see an amazing Buddhist temple? Then, you may want to visit the Kek Lok Si Temple in Penang on the west coast of West Malaysia. The name of the temple translates to the "temple of supreme bliss" and it is truly a spectacular sight.

It has hundreds of Buddha images and is the largest Buddhist temple in the country. The Temple of Rama IV is one of the highlights of the complex. It contains over ten thousand carvings of Buddha!

Semenggoh Nature Reserve

Would you like to see orangutans playing in the wild forest? Then, you may want to visit the Semenggoh Nature Reserve in the western section of East Malaysia. There, scientists bring rescued or orphaned orangutans and train them to survive in the wild.

YELLOW-RUMPED FLOWERPECKER

The surrounding forests are home to these interesting primates. The nature reserve is also home to many interesting Malaysian birds, such as the Malaysian honeyguide and the yellow-rumped flowerpecker.

Sipadan

Would you like to go diving and see lots of different sea creatures? Then, you may want to visit Sipadan, which is the only ocean island in the country. Sipadan is located on the eastern coast of East Malaysia and is surrounded by the Celebes Sea. One of the best diving spots worldwide, Sipadan has over 3,000 different fish species.

If you go diving there, you may come across a manta ray or large populations of silvery barracudas traveling together. You might see a hawksbill turtle or a green turtle swimming close by as you dive down into the coral that lives on top of an inactive volcano. When you come back to the surface, you can get out of the water and relax on the beautiful, sandy beach.

Petronas Twin Towers

Would you like to walk along a sky bridge between two towers? Then, you may want to visit the amazing Petronas Twin Towers in Malaysia's largest city of Kuala Lumpur. The towers are 88 floors in height and you can walk between the towers about halfway up. It's an amazing view of the city from there!

SUMMARY

The multicultural country of Malaysia is split into West and East landmasses with the South China Sea between them. Malaysia has only been an independent country since 1963 and it is still developing as a nation. For the amount of landmass that it has, most of Malaysia is sparsely populated. Malaysia has some of the world's most beautiful beaches and dense rainforests.

Awesome! Now that you've learned about and gone exploring in Malaysia, you may want to visit the city of Hong Kong in the Baby Professor book What Makes Little Hong Kong Big to the World? Geography Books for Third Grade.

Visit

BABY PROFESSOR
EDUCATION KIDS

www.BabyProfessorBooks.com

to download Free Baby Professor eBooks
and view our catalog of new and exciting
Children's Books